Simple Lean Manufacturing Principles

Simple Lean Manufacturing Principles

SPECIAL SECRET RESOURCE!

Lean Manufacturing - Incorporating It's Principles Into Your Business For Maximum Profits!

Are You Wondering How To Increase The Profits For Your Company? Looking For Efficient Methods To Increase Output, And Decrease Wastage? Want To Take Your Company's Growth To The Next Level, But Not Sure Where To Even Start?

Finally! You Now Have The All-in-one Lean Manufacturing Manual To Increase Your Profits To Unimaginable Levels... Discover The Time-tested Principles To Cut Down Costs, And Boost Productivity...and Get Visible Results!

AVAILABLE ONLY FOR A VERY LIMITED TIME!

"Discover a Powerful System You Can Use to Achieve Your Most Important Goals and Manage Your Time Effectively in Less than 1 Week"

Here's an Easy To Follow Step By Step System that will Show you The Time Management Secrets of the World's Most Successful People and Tell You Exactly How to Apply These Secrets in Your Life to Put Your Plans Into Action, Feel Proud of Your Accomplishments and Finally Experience Success

✓ **Eliminate Procrastination** Once in for all by Defining your Goals and Creating To Do Lists That Actually Work.

✓ **Achieve All Your Goals** by Setting Up Career, Family or Personal Goals That Mean the Most to You and Give You **Automatic Motivation Every time.**

✓ Achieve More **Success Easily at Work** by Producing **More Quality Results** in a Week Than Your Colleagues Can Produce in a Month.

✓ Spend **Quality Time With Your Family**, Play With Your Kids More Often And Feel More Satisfied and Recharged.

✓ **Reduce Mental Stress Easily**, You'll Go to Bed With the Feeling that You Have Done Your Best and Made Each and Every Minute Count. **No More Guilty Trips.**

✓ No More Running Around Like a Chicken With it's Head Cut off. Be in **Complete control of Your Time,** Your Life and Your Priorities.

✓ **Prioritize Your Schedule** according to what is most important and NEVER again push off the most important things to 'someday'.

✓ Divide up Your time for a **perfect Work, Play and Relax balance** that will recharge you and get you pumped up for **more success in your life**.

✓ Find **Time To Relax.** Find Time for Spa, Treat Your Self to a Golf Game With Your Buddies, Relax By the Beach...**Do Anything You Want.**

✓ Learn How to Never Get Sucked in By Old Habits and How to **Stay on Track** with Your Time Management No Matter What! (Time Sensitive FREE Bonus)

✓ And more..

Simple Lean Manufacturing Principles

Contents

What Is Lean Manufacturing?... 8
Lean Manufacturing Tools 10
Questions, Diagnostics And Assesments 12
Areas In Business Where Lean Can Help 14
5 Steps To Enable Lean Manufacturing Into Your Business 16
Lean Manufacturing And Consulting Firms In The UK 18
Definition Of Lean Manufacturing 21
Important Lean Manufacturing Terms : Definition 22
Lean Manufacturing Led Signs 23
Lean Manufacturing Consulting Ontario Canada 26
Lean Manufacturing Principles 29
Lean Manufacturing Processes 32
Lean Manufacturing Towards Success 35
Free Training On Lean Manufacturing 37
Lean Manufacturing In The UK 40
What Is Lean Manufacturing?.. 43
Companies That Use Lean Manufacturing With Success 46
Implementing Lean Manufacturing Systems 49
Lean Manufacturing Books 52
Lean Manufacturing Consultants 55
Implementing The Lean Manufacturing Strategy 58
Lean Manufacturing Printing Industry 60
Lean Manufacturing Six Sigma 63
The Benefits Of A Lean Manufacturing System 65
Move Ahead The Corporate Ladder With Lean Manufacturing Training 68
The Philosophy Of Lean Manufacturing 71
What Is Lean Manufacturing?.. 74
The Lean Manufacturing Process 77
Learning The Basics Of Lean Manufacturing And Processing 80
When Is A Change In Management Required In Lean Manufacturing?......................... 83
The Five Principles Of Lean Manufacturing 86

What Is Lean Manufacturing?

Why is Lean Manufacturing or thinking so prevalent in the modern current economies of scale? To remain competitive, agile and the lowest cost producers, providers and streamlined business, getting rid of waste and being highly, consistently and sustainable is key for survival and thriving in this new economy.

Lean manufacturing or thinking is exactly what the name sounds like - it is about 'cut to the bone', fat-trimmed, streamlining operation and organizations.

Authors Womack and Jones define lean thinking as a set or collection of 'efficiency tools' that you can unleash in your business to save money, reduce cost and waste and deliver consistent and effective service that is affordable and pleasing to your customers. It is about vision and tools for reducing variability and cutting down on waste, being efficient and running a smooth and competitive, even profitable operation, well.

The thinking was initially championed by pioneers like Toyota and it was eventually adopted by the Japanese automakers as the principle upon which they wanted to build, run and grow their businesses. Only a little later, will the Western world catch onto the value and potential of this approach to their respective organizations and operations.

Some have referred to lean manufacturing as the TOYOTA PRODUCTION SYSTEM, or JIT (just-in-time) manufacturing, paying attention to things like flow productions, line operations, value streams, Kaizen (which we will get to later). In any lean manufacturing process and approach there are a couple of things to pay attention to. There is discipline, planning, rigor, scientific approach and statistically-based tools required and applied to make this business paradigm fit, work and last.

Lean manufacturing will help you in your business take a serious look at visible causes and effects in your business. Aspects that could get some attention could include things like:

inventory
movement/motion

waiting or queues

broken machines or tools (missing)

dirt and clutter

noise

… and many others.

Things that we can see that is obvious waste or inefficiencies attract attention and demand action. This is where lean manufacturing steps in and makes the difference. It deals with the problems that we can actually SEE and do something about.

Lean Manufacturing Tools

Some of the lean manufacturing tools that might be able to help you in your processes are:

- 5S
- Cellular Manufacturing
- Mistake Proofing
- Set-Up Reduction

A basic fundamental tool in Lean manufacturing that can help any business the '5S' approach is an organizing, structuring technique to get rid of clutter and waste. Cleanliness and having a set place for everything is key.

The name stems from the Japanese meanings and equivalent words for…

- Sorting things (seiri)
- Setting things in a particular order (Seiton)
- Shining, daily maintenance (Seiso)
- Standardization (Seiketsu)
- Sustainability (shitsuke)

Cut costs and reduce waste by applying these simple techniques to your business today.

Cellular manufacturing has to do with organizing not the workplace only but the work as well. Work-cells and designated work- areas, certain spaces for certain activities, minimizes movement of people and things, therefore costing less. In an operational sense this means no batching, no waiting, no delays, no queuing, just smooth operation and easy flow.

Mistake-proofing (Poka-Yoke)

Built-in safeguards, reducing defects to zero is at the center of this approach. Highlighting problems as they occur, not letting mistakes, oversights and errors slip through is key.

Processes are designed around this principle to be more efficient and will help you business cut down on cost, scrap and waste.

(SMED or single minute exchange of dies) Quick and speedy change-over in business processes, manufacturing and operations are essential. Remember time and quality matters, means money! Process thinking is the key here. Getting rid of unnecessary steps, actions or movement are key. Reducing time on any line, saves money.

There is more to lean manufacturing that just these couple of tools. They just serve as an introduction to some of the major business enablers that LM can bring to your business and organization.

Questions, Diagnostics And Assesments

You can not change what you do not acknowledge or know about. Lean Manufacturing brings with the appeal and awareness to 'take note' and notice things around you (cost, waste, movement, clutter, scrap etc.) and then DO something real, meaningful and constructive about it!

What improvements should and could be made are both important questions to ask, prioritize and act upon. Customer priorities, things that affect your incoming revenue should get attention quickly and first. Things like quality, lead and waiting, cycle time, cost, inventory and other internal processes that affect the customer and are 'internal' and controllable, should be dealt with expediently.

In order to get you started asking the right type of questions could provide you with hints as to a strategy and starting point/priority:

Which process or step should get the bulk of our immediate attention –where is the biggest WIN-WIN for both the customer and the company? What are all the priorities that we need to pay attention to in this organization/business and operation, map the processes and make the list. Then ask in what order you should tackle the priorities? How do we get the BEST improvements the quickest way? How do/can we tap into the benefits of LM right away?

If reducing overhead, quality costs and inventory to save money, reduce weight and be a smooth operating, streamlined and cost-efficient provider are keys to your business success, LM can help your business in all aspects and areas.

Taking the theory of LM to the practical implementation will take planning, patience and persistence. Determination, detail orientation and discipline. We often refer to these as the THREE p's and the THREE d's to make them easy to remember. Gradual, planned, focused effort is what it is all about. Step-by-step instructions and actions to get to improvements over time, that can be sustained, stable and predictable are essential. If any of the following scenarios are important to your business, LM can help you reach targets and goals in this area that you set for you, your team and your business:

Lean Manufacturing Principles Made Easy

Increasing operating margin and revenue

Reduce manufacturing lead, wait and cycle times

Lessen WIP or work-in-progress inventory (half-completed product), time and space costs money! Reduce costs

Reducing manufacturing overhead and quality costs

Increase gross profit margin

Get customers what they want, when they want it, anytime, every time and all the time, quickly and correctly, affordably and on-demand.

Achieve consistent quality and low defect rate (scrap/waste)

Make the most of your shareholder value and you can not go wrong. Achieve high levels of improvement rates and customer satisfaction, quality products, low costs and do so quickly and you remain competitive and profitable.

Get and keep your processes under control and improve getting better all the time, setting and positioning yourself head-and-shoulders above the masses and mediocrity. Help define and execute your competitive edge with a well-thought out, supported, gradual deployment, throughout or LM in your business and you are set for desired outcomes, success and results!

Having a very real measurable impact and resulting dramatic improvements in your business listening to your customer complaints can give you great hints as to where some of the problems might lie. DO NOT hesitate to ASK them! They will tell you. It is a wonderful opportunity and channel to let your customers know that what they want, say and need, REALLY MATTERS. If you provide this level

Areas In Business Where Lean Can Help

Other aspects of lean to consider for LM deployment in your business are as follows:

Leadership

Initiative and leading by example from the top is key. The main flag-bearer and champion of this LM process and initiative starts with the business leader (CEO/President) and the senior management team. Buy-in and support can make or break the efforts of LM.

Personal, hands-on, practical engagement, commitment, practice and even reward for full participation in these initiatives, being the drivers of performance per se is critical to and for LM success. Inspire and mobilize others.

Corporate, business culture and infrastructure, support and championing of the LM efforts contribute to the momentum and success of it throughout the organization.

Include and engage EVERYONE! LM provides you the opportunity to harness and leverage the talents of the entire workforce and collective, not merely a hand-full of individuals or some employees. MAKE EVERYONE COUNT AND CONTRIBUTE!

If lasting results and sustained top performance matters to you and your business here are the means to that end in the LM toolkit!

Metrics and goals make things easier to achieve and practically act upon, effect, change, impact, reshape etc. MAKE EVERY ASPECT OF YOUR BUSINESS COUNT!

Infrastructure, support and deployment

Share the commitment, discipline and persistent toil to get to where you need to be. It starts with everyone, not just some! Have you customers front-of-mind at every step, process and corner of what you are doing, planning, improving, know what they value, why and how to get it to them quickly, effectively, consistently and affordably, anytime, every time! SHIFT YOUR FOCUS.

Shareholder value and $$ impact is a good guidelines for priorities and activity within LM. IMPROVEMENTS CAN/SHOULD BE MEASURABLE AND ACTAULLY TRACKED!

Engage everyone in the process, assign roles and responsibilities and tap into the full potential everyone has to bring to the table. Committed resources, time and training (initial investment) will pay off quickly. Mobilize your workforce and enable, empower and energize them.

5 Steps To Enable Lean Manufacturing Into Your Business

Here are 5 easy tips of how to enable LM in your organization:

1. Keep The Channels Of Communication Open

Talk and inform often

Educate and empower, knowledge, skill, practice and competence, on-going mastery and teaching others

Trust, honesty and information = transparency

Give everyone a head start, a common language, goal and purpose and unleash the power of lean on your organization.

2. Give Opportunity For Everyone For Input And Feedback

Get everyone engaged, excited and hands-on, involved and aboard with your LM initiative and plans

Introduce feedback and coaching, establishing communication channels where before they might have been none

3. Create And Cultivate The Right Working Context And Environement Where Honesty Is Always The Best Policy!

Set communication and information sharing, learning and openness (transparency) as an organizational priority

Less people will feel threatened and insecure about speaking up, hiding errors for fear of embarrassment or consequences (like being held accountable or losing their jobs or face in front of others)

Treat each other with respect and share ideas, issues openly, always keeping in mind the overall benefit (or detriment) for all if closer attention are paid to certain issues or challenges at hand.

4. Take Notice, Reward, Encourage And Celebrate!

Select examples of great achievement with LM, samples, project studies, specifics, general, share and celebrate them all-round. Give credit and recognition to the team where it is due, even for accomplishments that made a great difference for the company, a specific area or problem that was solved. It is highly motivational and quite an incentive for many to keep trying and even do more!

5. Implement A System And Metrics And Monitor Process BUT ALSO PROGRESS!!

Formalized record and tracking is essential for these LM processes and initiative to WORK and LAST! Ensure they are streamlines and purposeful, organized and regularly occur.

Lean Manufacturing And Consulting Firms In The UK

Today, every corporate industry has begun to rely heavily on lean manufacturing principles, so that they can deal with their varied day-to-day issues and crises.

This is the reason why many companies are working hard to produce huge profits. Today, generating savings and additional revenues, coupled with significant and high profits, keeps a company moving steadily forward.

UK is considered to be one among the most developed and highly progressing nationsin the global arena. Companies located here are found to be constantly aspiring to generate large savings.

Corporate ambience in the UK

As UK is among the highly progressive nations in the European Union, Brtish firms are working hard to put up with the intense and powerful competition. The corporate world has to face immense pressure from local corporations and firms also.

In order to cope up with this, it has become common for British companies to methodize, reconstruct and plan their efforts and daily operations with utmost care. Adding to the pressure is the increasing number of takeovers and aquisitons of companies, both large and small.

Firms are struggling to reduce the cost of operations which is the main cause behind the narrowed marginal profit of the company. Generation of savings is the main aim and objective of all local companies, not only in the UK, but in other nations too. By doing so, a high profit can be acheived by the firm and additional revenues can be gained.

Several UK based firms which had survived and excelled in the challenging economies of the past, are now giving in to the constantly increasing difficulties and global crises imposed by the corporate arena.

Lean Manufacturing

It is a term which refers to the strategies, principles and ideas that can be adopted by companies which are striving to cut down tremendous and aprreciably high operational costs.

Lean manufacturing makes use of innovative and creative ideas to fight against rising expenses involved in operational activities. It mainly targets reduction and elimination of wastes and unnecessary practices which are found to prevail widely in corporate industries.

Seven primary wastes need to be targeted and eliminated in all companies, not just firms based in UK, but firms in all nations. These wastes can be discarded by implementing the strategies and principles involved in lean manufacturing.

The following improvident activities have to be identified and overcome by adopting strategies of lean manufacturing :

Over production -- Every company in the UK is keen on reducing, or preferrably eliminating over production in its facilties. Over production results in piling up of inventories which eventually causes a preposterous and untimely drop in prices.

Over processing -- The principles of lean manufacturing are adopted by firms to cut down over processing, as it is the major contributor of unnecessary expenses which can be avoided. This is an activity which is not really essential and unavoidable for the operation of a company.

Over processing results in accumulation of wasteful activities and tasks in the firm. The principles of lean manufacturing are adopted by companies to rid over processing.

Transportation -- The hike in oil and petroleum prices is prevalent not only in Uk, but all over the world.

So companies in UK are focussing on lowering costs involved in transportation. It is surprising to note that a significant amount of funds can be saved by merely reducing costs involved in transportation requirements. Plenty of strategies and ideas are available, that will help the company to reduce transportation expenses.

Motion -- Employees need to have sufficient space to move around in the work area. This can be ensured by removal of useless equipments, which in turn will increase the speed of production. UK based companies are already focusing on giving the workers spacious working environment.

Inventory -- Piling up of inventories is undesirable in today's corporate world.as it becomes the firm's liability.

Waiting -- By using the strategies of lean manufacturing, waiting time can be eradicated and converted into useful, productive time. This fact is well known by UK companies.

Defects and scraps -- Lean manufacturing focuses on maximizing productivity and profits in the work environment. It helps the firms to avoid production of defective and erroneous products, thereby allowing the UK based firms to enjoy maximum benefits.

Consultancy firms in UK

There are plenty of firms dealing with lean manfacturing consultation situated in the UK, and also in most other countries. It just requires the human resource consultants to log online and learn more about the principles of lean manufacturing.

In the UK, firms dealing with lean manufacturing consultation have developed theri own industry.

Definition Of Lean Manufacturing

It does not take a rocket scientist to understand the meaning of Lean Manufacturing, nor does it take a group of experts to comprehend its basic idea and concepts. It simply refers to the achievement of the maximum profit and efficiency that a company is capable of by eradicating wasteful events and activites that commonly exist in a corporate regime.

At first, some firms adopt Lean Manufacturing ideas in their manufacturing processes because it has a fancy name. But truthfully, it is actually a lot simpler than it sounds. What is essentially required to achieve good results through lean manufacturing, is a true form of committment and discipline to bring about significant change in the results of the company.

First, let us begin by locating the top seven wastes that companies diagnosed as the top reasons behind delay in production, massive costs, filings of bankruptcy and ultimately, hostile takeovers in corporate firms. They are :

1) Overproduction
2) Inventory
3) Transportation
4) Processing
5) Motion (Processes that can be avoided)
6) Waiting time
7) Defects in Manufacturing

These are the prime reasons that often contribute to the failure of a firm. For instance, instead of looking at quicker and more cost effective ways of producing high quality output, these firms waste time and funds in fixing equipment, manufacturing defects, and other hitches. If the problem had been dealt with in the very beginning, such wasteful activities would have been avoided completely.

Lean Manufacturing Principles Made Easy

Important Lean Manufacturing Terms : Definition

A company that is interested in understanding Lean Manufacturing techniques thoroughly, must make itself familiar with the official terms connected with the concept. These words must not scare you away.

Cellular Manufacturing

In cellular manufacturing, manual operations and machine operations are linked to produce efficient and excellent results economically and in a cost-efficient manner. It is also designed to extract highest possible value from a method and activity performed. It reduces wastes side by side. Cellular manufacturing adopts a U-shaped pattern and has a single flow direction.

Kanban System

It adopts a pull method in which colour coded cards are connected to parts to ensure smooth flow of production process. The 'pull method' just indicates that the interest of the consumer is of top priority instead of what you, the manufacturer, desires.

Value

Value refers to what the consumer is ready to pay for your services. Lean Manufacturing strategies hold complete responsibility of satisfying the requirements of the customer accurately.

Pull System

It involves the replenishment of depleted and used goods only.

Takt Time

Takt time is valued based on the customers' demand. Takt time sets the speed of production depending on how desperately the customers require the product. It is commonly known as the heart beat of lean manufacturing systems.

Lean Manufacturing Led Signs

Systems and processes connected with lean manufacturing, require LED signs or display boards so that the process flow within the organisation can be monitored and adjusted as per the requirement.

The lean manufacturing system has ideas and principles that were introduced by Japanese. They have achieved worldwide recognition and are so renowned that it is highly probable that even the common man may have come across it, or even be indirectly involved in some form of lean manufacturing.

The purpose of implementing lean manufacturing in a firm is to divide the workforce into distinct divisions that can be monitored and controlled easily. Companies which have adopted lean manufacturing strategies and schemes must understand the necessity of mapping and measuring each and every stage of the available value for every product with the main objective bring elimination and reduction of wastes from all the systems and processes.

Using LED signs coupled with lean manufacturing will enhance the lean manufacturing programs of the company. These LED signs will rapidly improve the efficiency and effectiveness of existing programs by providing the company with the abilities to accurately post measurements in locations where they have high demand.

The following are some of the LED signs that are available:

1. Plant efficiency data that is displayed by Alpha 7120.
2. Overall shipping performance that is displayed by Alpha 9240
3. Productivity information that is displayed by AlphaVision PC.

A company can achieve the targets listed below by using LED signs of lean manufacturing:

1. Cycle time reduction by about 40% - 50%
2. Set up time reduction by about 25% - 35%
3. Down time reduction by about 35% - 45%

4. Over all productivity improvement by about 30% - 40%
5. WIP reduction by about 25% - 35%
6. Scrap reduction by about 35% - 45%
7. Travel distance reduction by about 40% - 80%
8. Floor space reduction by about 20% - 30%

Firms that are thoroughly engaged in usage of lean manufacturing systems or programs need to have the LED signs of lean manufacturing in order to achieve similar results.

Key Principles of Lean Manufacturing

1. Throught Lean Manufacturing, the value is defined precisely from the point of view of the final consumer.

2. The value stream is identified entirely for each product line and wastes are eliminated.

3. The smooth flow of value added activites is ensured by lean manfacturing.

4. The customer's needs are satisfied by lean manufacturing, only upon the request of the customer.

5. Through continuous improvement, lean manufacturing principles pursure perfection in every activity.

Cornerstones of Efficient Lean Manufacturing Program

1. Creation of an Exciting Culture. An exciting and enterprising culture is created by using LED signs of lean manufacturing.

2. Empowerment of Participative environment. The employees of corporate firms are encouraged to participate in the constantly improving lean manufacturing systems and processes, by using LED signs of lean manufacturing.

3. A distinct visual measurement is provided through the usage of LED signs of lean manufacturing.

4. Organizing a visual and disciplined work environment. Thebusiness firm can be promoted to greater heights by the usage of LED signs of lean manufacturing.

5. Encouraging steady and constant improvement of the study environment. It is possible to create a continuously imporving environment by applying LED signs of lean manufacturing.

Visual Workplace Solutions - Meaning

This has been considered by manufacturing industries. How much have they spent on different processes and equipment, just to produce impressive and effective reports that will undergo reviewing after a fact? LED signs of lean manufacturing will ensure that the key points of various reports are reachable by employess and firms that have a desperate and instant need for them.

By supporting the main principles of lean manufacturing, several LED sign manufacturers have come up with a whole new line or series of such LED signs of lean manufacturing . These LED signs are called Visual Workplace Solutions (VWS) and are designed especially to supply extremely high lean manufacturnig performance to establishments and employees that have maximum requirement for them.

The LED signs of lean manufacturing serve as the scoreboards which indicate the performance of a company and give a clear picture of tremendous gains in a competitive environment.

LED Signs of Lean Manufacturing: Performance Scores and Metrics

The organisation must put forth the right data to the employees and concerned people so that it yields immediate and accurate results, and improving the morale of the people simultaneously.

Lean Manufacturing Consulting Ontario Canada

Companies and local firms situated in Ontario, Canada, one of the economic capitals of the world, are constantly working towards making their operations more efficient.

As the present times are dire and the prices of energy sources control the operations of large businesses, lean manufacturing has made itself indispensable to every company that is in distress.

Just like every other economic city, companies and firms in Ontario are primarily aiming at reducing costs, generating savings and producing maximum margin of profit.

As the competitition among industries and also, inter-industries, has become very intense, every business faces the challenge of bettering their competitiveness, as the very first step.

Enumerous businesses and firms are put up in Ontario, Canada. The firms which are based here undergo extreme pressure due to the intense business environment that prevails there.

This is why, lean manufacturing consultancy has become a flourishing industry in Ontario, Canada. With so many companies that are in distress, lean manufacturing strategies are becoming the governing guidleines in their everyday operations.

Consulting firms

The number of companies that specialize in lean management advise is constantly increasing in Ontario, Canada.

The above mentioned consultancy firms collect fees for the advice they provide to their clients, in their respective fields and initiatives for increasing productivity and strength of competitiveness in their business.

The techniques of lean manufacturing have become excellent solutions for Ontario, Canada-based firms that are nearing the verge of closing or inefficiency.

Locating the best consulting firm based in Ontario

Locating the ideal consulting firm proves to be a real challenge to a company, that needs to streamline and rationalise its operations at the earliest.

Since all companies in Ontario are trying to achieve goals concerning high efficiency, consulting firms specialising in lean manufacturing are showing a greatly improving, lucrative performance as the days go by.

Companies must show utmost concentration in order to locate the perfect consulting firm that will provide ideal tips on lean manufacturing.

However, it is very difficult to find consulting and advisory firms which will provide its services for low fees, if the company is focussed on saving.

Hence, it is recommended that companies should focus and plan clearly, before undertaking implementation of lean manufacturing techniques.

Planning takes up a lot of time and work. But it is worthwhile as it makes the implementation of the principles very easy and produces effective results.

Finding the perfect consulting firm in Ontario, is similar to going shopping. As they are many firms that deal with lean manufacturing advisory. the rates may vary from firm to firm.

In order to finalise the best deal for your business, it is important that you, as a scheming and resourceful manager, compare the rates offered by different firms. When such a comparative study is done, your company is bound to obtain the best deal for the services from the consulting firm.

This is equivalent to maximizing the benefits of lean manufacturing.

While looking for consulting services. the next best thing that you can do is to take feedback and advice from the past experiences of peers and other companies.

Experience is very convincing and is always the best teacher. Hence, learning from the past experiences of other companies will definitely prove to be useful and valuable in all cases.

In Ontario, many companies are implementing the techniques of lean manufacturing. It is a good idea to find out about their experience in seeking advise from consulting companies in Ontario, as it will provide a clear picture of what you must expect.

It is said that wise men gain knowledge from the experience of those around them, and not from their own personal experience. It is recommended that you observe very carefully before taking any steps of your own if your company is based in Ontario, Canada.

Lean manufacturing schemes require ardent and religious implementation of the principles governing lean manufacturing.

Lean Manufacturing Principles

Understanding the Principles of Lean Manufacturing

Companies are constantly striving to run their businesses more efficiently. The most common way of beating competition is to reduce costs drastically. By practicing the principles of lean manufacturing, this efficient management setting is achieved.

Lean Manufacturing promotes the philosophy of eliminating wastes in a company. It focuses on reducing the top seven wastes that exist in any manufacturing unit or business. The common wastes are over processing, transportation, waiting time, motion, scrap, inventory and over production.

The principles of lean manufacturing provide the necessary help and guidelines to any company that wishes to produce the best results that it is capable of. These principles are adopted to create a work environment that is productive, be it a factory, a warehouse, or even an office.

Perfect Time

Producing perfect quality right at the beginning, is the most important priority of lean manufacturing principles. We can reach maximum efficiency by avoiding the time that goes into quality inspection, once the production process has been completed.

How can we achieve ideal first time quality? This can be done by dealing with problems at the very beginning. After a thorough analysis of the normal production process, the wastes and inefficiencies involved, can be identified. Following this, these defects can be solved in a step by step process.

The final result of adopting this principle of lean manufacturing is that absolutely no time is wasted in inspecting the quality of goods produced or company errors as all the difficulties and problems are dealt with, way before they become a prominent issue for the company.

Waste reduction

The second important principle involved in lean manufaturing strategy is minimising the waste. It suggests that wasteful activities which do not add to the significant improvement of the company, be eliminated. So, the company's resources(land, capital and people) are made use of efficiently.

This does not necessarily mean reduction of the number of workers, but they can be shifted to departments in which their skills are utilized thoroughly. This principle of lean manufacturing is a very common excuse offered by companies which remove learge number of workers. But waste minimization is foun d to be highly effective when used within the corporate regime.

Pursuing best results

The third principle of lean manufacturing is perpetual improvement. As the name suggests, this principle looks at endless ways that will contribute to the improvement of the company. Some examples of this principle include cost reduction, ideal ways of performing a task, and production of best quality output. If proven suggestions, that can make the process more effective, are provided, they should be readily adopted. Tested knowledge and accurate information form the back bone of lean manufacturing principles.

Flexing your Muscles

Flexibility is the fourth principle of lean manufacturing techniques. The managament needs foresight and keen observing capacity of the trends in the market. Flexibility refers to producing a diversified mix of products rapidly without making any sacrifice in the quality of the product, even when production is in a small scale.

How can one follow these principles of lean manufacturing? One must have a clear business plan and must closely monitor the market. The plan should be flexible so that it can adapt to increase in production volume or introduction of a new product line. By expecting things that are least expected, and by handling the situaion with grace, the principles of lean manufacturing can be handled efficiently.

Pull not Push

The fifth principle of lean manufacturing is Pull processing. It means that products must not be pushed from the end where production takes place, instead, they must be pulled from the consumer's end.

All about relationships

The last principle of lean manufacturing focuses on creating and maintaining a strong, healthy relationship with the company's partners and suppliers, using tactics like information sharing arrangements, risk and cost sharing.

By adopting such methods, both the companies will grow steadily and simultaneously. Thought this last principle may sound odd, collaborating with suppliers and partners enables your company to achieve greater heights, and operate effiiciently, with the additional possibilty of increasing job opportunities

Following these principles of lean manufacturing doesn not imply that a more productive organization will be formed. The implementation of these principles is just as important as holding the map. Creating a clear plan and also its effective execution can strengthen or reduce the effectiveness of the above mentioned principles of lean manufacturing.

Lean Manufacturing Processes

Understanding the Processes of Lean Manufacturing

Inspiring and promoting companies to adopt strategies that would improve the benefits and value of their products and services, and simultaneously reducing wasteful activities and operations, is the most important objective that applies to lean manufacturing processes.

Ever since its introduction. experts say that it was developed by business magnate Henry Ford and further popularised by Toyota. All companies are fascinated by what the processes involved in lean manufacturing can do for their business.

For companies that have already adopted lean manufacturing systems, the processes have turned out to be a tremendous success and highly beneficical to companies and their respctive workforces.

Processes adopted by the Workforce

Workers are undoubtedly considered to be the major elements in the line of manufacturing. By implementing lean manufacturing processes, employees are greatly benefited as the workload is reduced by a significant amount and the burden is made less taxing.

The main principle behind processes in lean manufacturing is reducing and eradicating wastes from the industrial setting. Waiting time is one of the prominent wasteful activities. When the employees note a reduction in waiting time, productivity is increased and work environment becomes more positive. A positive environment leads to extremely positive results.

Processes for Customers

Consumers are ready to pay only for services that will be value for their capital.

Processes involved in lean manufacturing focus on satisfying the consumer's needs accurately. This system enables the manufacturer to keep the customer's needs and best interests as the vital point. The clients are extremely happy when the company gives them their top priority.

Businesses conduct surveys and studies to determine what the customer's needs are. Using these survey results, the company will begin working on their available resources and energy sources to accomplish the task.

Processes for the company

Companies will achieve great advantages from these processes because it focuses on reducing costs and achieveing maximum output. The term 'lean' means just that. Supplying the required goods, at the specified time, at the place of demand and in appropriate amounts.

Hence, no surplus. No excessive production. No piling up of inventories. By endorsing lean manufacturing processes, the firm can be sure of absolutely no wastage at an production level.

The top seven wastes that have been commonly identified in firms are:

- inventory
- transportation
- waiting time
- defects
- motion
- overproduction
- underutilized workforce

These wastes must be eradicated to ensure that the company utilises its potential to the maximum benefit. They have been identified by firms all around the world and account for low production and less efficiency. Lean manufacturing processes focus on eliminating these wasteful activities.

Experts often feel that lean manufacturing is an expensive strategy when applied to companies that have been operating for a long period of time. But when the idea is given a deeper thought, you will realise that the initial expenses made by the firm gets compensated by the high profits produced in the long run.

Adopting lean manufacturing strategies is a risk. But we must not let ourselves be forced to continue with the age-old, primitive ideas just to be free from risks of all kinds, when we have proof of what lean manufacturing techniques can do for the betterment of the company.

Lean Manufacturing Towards Success

Simply put, Lean manufacturing endorses the 'no waste' principle in the management of the workplace and in production activities. It functions irrespective of company size. It does not matter if it is a large corporate regime or a small team of five women managing a cookie business, but, the success of lean manufacturing strategy lies in the effective execution and organization of those involved in it.

Observers say that the Japanese were the first to popularize lean manufacturing strategy. Japan is a country renowned for its highly innovative principles and creative approaches to various methods, including problem-solving techniques.

The principles of lean manufacturing border practicality and simplicity. Though the concept is easy to understand and implement, it is equally important that the right attitude and approach is maintained throughout the program.

As lean manufacturing principles have proved highly successful in the case of large corporations like Toyota, several other firms are now determined to apply these techniques to their own businesses.

With the increasing prices of energy sources, and intensifying business competition, firms are striving hard to reduce operational costs. Many companies are filing bankruptcy in the Chapter 11 of business journals and mismanagement has been identified as the most common reason behind it. Many stable companies have also been affected. This is where lean manufacturing principles help companies that wish to recover.

Depending on how a company initiates deals and achieves maximum profits from the existing resources, we can judge the success of the lean manufacturing strategy. Success is also determined by reducing, and gradually eliminating wasteful activities that are commonly found in many corporate environments.

Some of the wastes that have been identified are: Transportation (movement of goods in excess to the minimum requirement), motion (employees who work more than necessary), defects (inspection and fixing of problems), over processing (conducting excess work), over production (piling up of stocks) and inventory.

When a firm produces a product in excess, it is probable that the product will be sold at a much lower price than what was intended. The manufacturer is pressured to sell all the goods and hence, forced to dispose the products at record low prices.

A company which has efficiently implemented the principles of lean manufacturing will not undergo this. It will create a production level that is sufficient and will accurately deliver the results as and when required. There will be no time wastage, or over production.

From the customer's point of view, it is beneficial as their needs are satisfied effectively. From the manufacturer's point of view also lean manufacturing creates positive results, because there is no wastage or resources, energy or time.

As mentioned earlier, success in lean manufacturing principles depends entirely on the way it is adopted and implemented. Simply put, it is up to you. Before adopting the ideas and methods of Lean manufacturing, careful planning is a must. If the process is taken up in a haphazard and reckless manner, without bothering about the probable consequences, the entire effort proves pointless.

Free Training On Lean Manufacturing

Lean manufacturing is comprehensive and efficient set of principles, ideas and business strategies which are aimed at maximizing productivity by significantly reducing wasteful, unproductive and worthless tasks, elements and activities that are prevalent in work places.

Most companies suffer from problems relating to labour relations and concerns, which affect the alliance between workers and employers, eventually causing an ill effect on the production activities of the firm.

Owing to challenging situations along with various crises affecting society, political environment, industrial and corporate regimes, companies around the world are beginning to suffer from low profits and narrowed margins.

Problems in Labor relations have become very common among industries worldwide. Companies from every field have started announcing job cuts, organising activities, streamlining and reconstructing efforts in every division.

Hence, productivity, both from the company as well as from the workers, should be enhanced and boosted to significant levels to ensure that the industry survives all drawbacks.

Lean Manufacturing

Industries all over the world are realising the benefits of adopting and implementing effective business strategies and techniques that will successfully support the survival of the firm.

The Japanese are pioneers in creating innovative, yet practical, strategies, principles and business techniques that will ensure business improvement. They have never failed, be it in the industrialization era of the 1980s or the modern era of the 1990s, till date.

Analysts could not identify the exact origin of lean manufacturing methodologies and concepts, but they have strong belief that it is related to the working guide of Japanese 5S.

5S helps in eradication of unnecessary and wasteful events by establishing discipline, cleanliness and effective organisation of processes in the workplace. This is quite similar to the concepts dealt in lean manufacturing.

Learning more about principles of lean manufacturing

There are various methods and means by which managers, employees and workers of a firm can efficiently learn and understand the techniques of lean manufacturing systems.

There are several training and consultancy firms that offer long and short term programs on lean manufacturing strategies.

You must note that these training programs are quite expensive. But the corresponding reduction and cost effectiveness that wil be produced by efficiently implementing these techniques will more than compensate for the training expense.

Nowadays, companies are looking at lean manufacturing trainings as one among the vital areas where investment and capital can be spent lavishly.

There are several online sites that provide training programs on lean manufacturing, but they are rarely available for free. This is because the lean manufacturing training industry is a flourishing one, and brings in huge profits.

Free Training

Locating an online site which offers free lean manufacturing training is practically impossible.

Several firms and companies that have an upper hand on lean manufacturing strategies, have realised their demand in today's corporate environment. It has opened new opportunities to earn and generate additonal income.

Since the principles and strategies of lean manufacturing have become an essential requirement for companies striving to improve production and efficiency, free training programs have become an unachievable dream.

As free training program for lean manufacturing concepts is not available online or in personal consultancies, companies are ready to invest in it by sending main employees to expensive and paid training programs.

Following this, the employees who have attended the training program are expected to communicate the message connected to lean manufacturing principles, to the remaning staff.

This is a common practice in companies which are keen on lowering costs and operational expenditure.

By using this method, the training program is made free for the remaining employees.

Free Training on lean manufacturing, an impossible dream?

Since most industries around the globe are striving hard and focusing on survival in these troubled occasions, free training on the strategies of lean manufacturing has mild hope.

As most experts and pioneers in the field of lean manufacturing are making money out of their expertise, free training programs on lean manufacturing strategies seems like an impossible dream, unless interrupted by the government.

Governments all over the world, are striving to protect their economy by ensuring that their people have jobs, and by focusing on providing support to local businesses which may be on the verge of bankruptcy.

On account of these reasons, the government is expected to subsidize lean manufacturing training costs, by making them free for firms to understadn and implement.

It is definitely bound to happen sometime in the near future.

Lean Manufacturing In The UK

Introduction

The system of Lean manufacturing is the process or methodology of studying the scheme of flow of materials and elements in a productive environment. The system of lean manufacturing must be constantly upgraded through dedicated labor so that the enhanced output of the company can be achieved using the process itself.

Origin of Lean Manufacturing

Lean manufacturing systems in UK are quite similar to the lean manufacturing process in other nations. The lean manufacturing process that came into existence in North America, may have originated from the system of lean manufacturing that was practised in Toyota, Japan.

It is a well known fact and is not implausible that the system of lean manufacturing followed in UK have terms similar to that practised in North America and Japan. Several Japanese words are imbibed in the lean manufacturing process that are practised in other countries. Words sucha as kaizen, andon and kanban are undoubtedly and explicitly derived from the Japanese language.

Adopting Lean Manufacturing in UK

In UK also, the system of lean manufacturing endorses excellence that provides additional value to products and the removal of wasteful and useless activities also called as non-value adding activities, which is found to be similar to the process of lean manufacturing followed in other countries.

The principles of lean manufacturing that have been adopted in the UK, focus on controlling and monitoring the existing flow of goods production in line with the needs and demands of the consumer.

Lean Manufacturing Principles Made Easy

The following steps are followed as the building blocks which help in efficient operation of the systems and processes of lean manufacturing.

1. In order to achieve significant and predictable results, work must be standardized so that the operations will be streamlined and organised efficiently. This is one of the methods of lean manufacturing techniques.

2. The system of lean manufacturing uses work place management so that the flow and movement of operations can be monitored within the company. Looping and other tiring processes are seen as an obstacle in the company's path of betterment.

3. The techniques involved in lean manufacturing visually controls the proper organisation of processes within the company. Maintenance and control of process flow is well adapted to visual monitoring so that the workers can follow its actions easily.

4. In UK, Lean manufacturing portrays an effective layout of the industrial plant, so that effective ways of facilitating smooth flow of processes, and managing new concepts and configuration of the equipment.

5. In UK, Lean Manufacturing also focuses on inspection of product and equipment quality at the source. This can be facilitated by checking on resources and raw materials, which will effectively result in the production of superior goods.

6. In UK, lean manufacturing uses batch reduction technique, which concentrates on reducing and eliminating wastes that are prevalent in every batch that is manufactured.

7. In UK, lean manufacturing principles and systems form teams or work forces that can meet deadlines and solve problems by planning and streamlining activities.

8. In UK, lean manufacturing focuses on manufacturing products based on the demand from the customer. This is because the main aim of lean manufacturing is to utilize resources and energy sensibly so that it can produce results that are of significant value to the customers.

9. In UK, lean manufacturing works on a one-piece flow method. The process of one-piece flow is vital in adjusting and monitoring manufacturing processes that are already existing in a company. One-piece flow depends on continuity of a process and further reduction of complex and difficult processes will enhance the manufacturing system in a significant manner.

10. In UK, the system of lean manufacturing makes use of takt time. Takt time refers to the rate of demand imposed by the customer. Takt time determines the speed of the production activity so that it matches the demands and requirements of the customer accurately. Consequently, takt time is referred to as the heart beat of a manufacturing system.

Takt time is measured as the ratio of the available, existing work time to the sum of the units that have been sold.

What Is Lean Manufacturing?

Introduction

Lean Manufacturing is referred to as a form of prolonged improvement and when a company chooses to adopt its principles and strategies, a full-time regular improvement person should be appointed along with a regular improvement team.

Then, the firm will hire an expert consultant who will clearly map the operations of the company and point out specific areas where there is a need to improve.

Lean Manufacturing Terms: Definition

If a company desires to understand the concept of lean manufacturing, some terms have to be clearly defined. Some of the important terms connected with lean manufacturing have been listed below:

1. Value refers to what the potential customer is ready to pay for. In a company, a lean manufacturing process does exactly that, by satisfying the needs of the consumer efficiently.

2. The inter linking of manual and machine operations is called Cellular Manufacturing. It focuses on producing effective combinations that will maximize the value of activities, and simultaneously reducing wasteful activities which bug the company. This is the responsibility of the lean manufacturing strategy adopted by a company.

The layout of the cell is generally U-shaped and works on a one-piece flow system.

3. The Kanbam system works on a pull system which utilises cards which are color coded and attached to some parts of the container so that they can regulate the improvement in production and the flow of delivery processes. This is also an important reason why several companies have adopted lean manufacturing strategies.

4. Lean manufacturing refers to the process of analysing flow of materials and information in a productive environment by constantly improvising the system so that the company can achieve and deliver enhanced products to the consumer. Here, lean manufacturing process tries to accomplish streamlining of the existing manufacturing activities and also to increase the revenue gain.

5. If a lean manufaturing process locates an activitiy that doesn not add value, it will label it as a waste. A wasteful activity is a process that is not productive in any way, and is simply unnecessary. The principles of Lean manufacturing target at reducing and eliminating such wastes.

This is exactly the purpose of lean manufacturing, as it reduces, if not eradicating completely, unwanted and unnecessary activities by labeling them as wastes.

6. The Pull system is a form of controlling and monitoring the flow of information and resources by replenishing goods that have been depleted. Thus they are refilled. Here, lean manufacturing aims to create a systematic process of replacing depleted goods in the inventories.

7. The resources of a company are delivered to the customer after conducting surveys, forecasting and scheduling, using the Push system. Lean manufacturing works towards neglecting and disregarding the push system.

8. Takt time refers to the rate of demand for the products required by the customer. It aims at determining the speed or pace at which production of goods must take place in order to meet the requirements of the consumer. Takt time is referred to as the heartbeat of a manufacturing system. Lean manufacturing focuses on calculating this takt time.

Takt time is manipulated by determining the value of the ratio between the available work time to the total sum of the number of units that have been sold.

9. An added-value activity is a process that is targeted at improving the market trends, the function and service offered by the product. Basically, this refers to the value that had been mentioned in number one. Here, lean manufacturing focuses on guiding the manufacturing company into pouring their efforts towards the welfare and betterment of the company.

In the end, lean manufacturing focuses on complete, all-round improvement of the firm and the manufacturng process. Manufacturing processes of a company have always been, and will always continue to be, the part where constant and ceaseless efforts must be put in onreder to make progress. Hence, the last principle of a system involving lean manufacturing strategies, is constant and steady improvement. The principles and concepts of lean manufacturing have been a great source of inspiration to the remaining parts of the company as well.

Companies That Use Lean Manufacturing With Success

Success in the Implementation of Lean Manufacturing Principles in Companies

Lean manufacturing is a holistic and innovative approach to making companies' profits and earnings somehow upbeat and at par with contemporaries around the world.

Lean manufacturing, according to experts, was developed and initially implemented and launched in Japan, which is a country foremost known for interactive and inventive approaches to solving and dealing with problems.

Experts also note that lean manufacturing principles are very simple and practical. However, the success of lean manufacturing adoption and implementation depends and principally relies on the effective and religious implementation of the simple and easy to do strategic principles.

Lean manufacturing and companies

Companies around the world, in all aspects and in all industries, are now addressing lean manufacturing issues and concerns, one way or another. The fact that all companies need to reduce operation costs and expenses make up to the companies ever- enduring efforts and initiatives to adopt lean manufacturing principles.

There are numerous companies that fall and file for bankruptcy every now and then. The corporate world is alarmed because even the staunchest and most stable companies in the past decades are beginning to show signs and indications of deterioration and weakness nowadays.

It can be because the world economy is so challenged by the greatest problem that has bugged the economy of the world---rising and higher oil prices. Lea manufacturing is becoming very popular among all companies because of that.

Lean manufacturing principally aims to help companies by targeting or initiating ways, measures and practices that alleviate and reduce wasteful practices and behaviors in the work environment.

Lean manufacturing is also helping companies around the world to cope up with the real and emerging challenges in the real world when prices and costs are so volatile and influential to modern living and economies.

There are seven waste, wasteful practices and unproductive processes that lean manufacturing aims principally to erase or alleviate.

First, lean manufacturing aims to scrap over production among companies. Over production leads to lowering and declining prices of products and merchandise that would eventually lead to a company loss.

Second, lean manufacturing aims to reduce and cut over processing inside all companies. Over processing makes expenses higher by putting up additional costs and expenses for processing materials and labor costs. Time is also wasted by that.

Third, lean manufacturing maximizes transportation. You know that transportation is facilitated by automotive and cars. These in turn, burn up oil and petroleum that are currently priced at unreasonable levels.

Fourth, lean manufacturing makes motion productive. By eliminating wastes and setting aside big and space-consuming equipment in the work place, laborers are able to move freely, enabling them to eventually speed up production and do more outputs.

Fifth, lean manufacturing prevents piling up of inventories. In some industries, piled up inventories are positive, but in almost all, or the majority of manufacturing firms, inventories should be kept controlled because prices of the goods are affected by piled up inventories.

Lean manufacturing makes up operations streamlined and more efficient. Thus, for the sixth spot, lean manufacturing principles help make companies alleviate and prevent waiting time.

Lastly, because the environment is cleared from all obstacles and disturbance, lean manufacturing helps companies avoid the production of goods with scraps and defects.

Companies producing merchandise and outputs with scraps and defects not only suffer from losses from the production of such substandard products, they also lose customers because their credibility are destroyed and tainted.

Companies that successfully implement lean manufacturing principles

There are more and more companies around the world that successfully implement lean manufacturing techniques and principles in their daily operation.

It should be noted that companies that use lean manufacturing with success are characterized by one and a single unifying feature--- all of them are profitable and strong.

Companies that use lean manufacturing with success are also notably very competitive amid intense and rising competition in the corporate world.

Implementing Lean Manufacturing Systems

Lean manufacturing is a very good and effective concept of managing a company. The philosophy of reducing wastes found in a manufacturing business or any type corporation is a sound idea. The most common wastes that needs attention are:

- Overproduction
- Waiting time
- Transportation
- Processing
- Inventory
- Motion
- Scrap

When these wastes are minimized, the quality of the products or services is improved, the production time and the cost of manufacturing the goods is reduced. With this in mind, many companies go through lean manufacturing training to get the most out of their systems.

The goal of lean manufacturing for any business is to have the production and demand be linked directly. The result is a more efficient way in delivering your goods to the customer because you produce the product at the time the customer wants it. But this is only achieved if there is a proper implementing lean manufacturing guideline.

However, despite the training and guidelines, some companies have trouble in implementing lean manufacturing systems. There are different reasons in the failure of implementing lean manufacturing principles in projects. One of them is the difficulty in grasping the true nature lean manufacturing.

The most accepted form of implementing lean manufacturing is the kaizen. Kaizen in Japanese means, "improvement." In implementing lean manufacturing, kaizen can be done in large scale or small-scale projects. The most commonly used kaizen are the blitz events. These are short-term programs launched to instantly improve the production process.

Lean Manufacturing Principles Made Easy

Though kaizen is highly prized as a valuable tool in implementing lean manufacturing in a company, it is not enough. If an endless cycle of kaizen events is the only form of lean manufacturing tool used, the company may suffer. Why? Because blitz events can be expensive and may cost the organization more money in implementing it.

There are other implementing lean manufacturing tools that an organization can use to get the improvements they want. There is the Value Streaming and Process Mapping. These two can effectively eliminate waste and in implementing lean manufacturing, they can streamline work processes.

Although lean manufacturing may sound simple enough, there are companies that do not view it that way. They find implementing lean manufacturing obscure and cloudy. This means that they do not fully grasp the principles of lean manufacturing. The best solution is to hire a lean manufacturing consultant.

Once the consultant has made an assessment of the organization's problem areas, he can then suggest the most appropriate projects that will achieve the goals of the company. While the implementing lean manufacturing systems are explained to the managers and lean masters, the process of enforcing these systems and plans fall on the latter's shoulders.

For the company to fully appreciate the benefits of implementing lean manufacturing systems, they must be willing to wait. Change does not happen overnight and some resistance should be expected from the people directly affected by the implementing lean manufacturing systems.

Why is there resistance when lean manufacturing aims to improve the production quality of the organization? Simply put, some people hate change. They have been doing the same thing and have been used to going through the routine for years that it has almost become something familiar to them.

In light of this, companies should make it a point to clearly explain the changes in implementing lean manufacturing systems. If all things go smoothly for the first run, the implementing lean manufacturing system must be adopted as soon as possible to make sure that the workers do not forget the new process.

When implementing lean manufacturing systems involving the executive management, it is important to note that this group is the one that must have a full understanding of lean manufacturing principles. Their training must cover all disciplines of lean manufacturing including the planning and implementation tools.

Although lean manufacturing is one of the best choices for improving a company or organization, you must be certain if your business fits this philosophy. Not all the implementing lean manufacturing systems may be good for your business, like excessive use of the kaizen events.

In implementing lean manufacturing systems, most often the best way to employ its principles is by only taking the elements that fit your company. This way you also save money without losing valuable resources.

Lean Manufacturing Books

Lean manufacturing is the emerging trend nowadays for maximization of productivity among companies and firms.

Because today's time is so hard, with almost every company around the world suffering from narrowing margins and operation losses, major and established giant firms acknowledge and start implementing lean manufacturing strategies within their businesses.

However, lean manufacturing is a discipline, an approach that should be carefully studied before implemented in the workplace. Taking a closer look at it and its operational nature will ensure the attainment of desired benefits from lean manufacturing.

Because lean manufacturing is a helpful set of strategies and business operational techniques, it would be helpful if managers, employers, entrepreneurs and even the most common workers know about it.

In this regard, here are some of the best and most helpful books that are recommended if you want to study, look at and know more about lean manufacturing.

These books are available on your nearest book stands. These lean manufacturing books are also available online, so log in and check them out through your reliable and favorite online shopping Web site.

"5 Pillars of the Visual Workplace"

A book authored by Japanese expert Hiroyuki Hirano and translated by Bruce Talbot, "5 Pillars of the Visual Workplace" gives pertinent outlook and information about the visual workplace.

"5 Pillars of the Visual Workplace" touches and focuses on the widely popular 5S's principle, which are being used currently worldwide. These are seiri or organization, seiton or orderliness, seiso or cleanliness, seiketsu or standardized cleanup and shitsuke or discipline.

The Japanese 5S clearly and obviously outlines the approaches behind the ever-reliable lean manufacturing techniques. Apparently, the two workplace concepts are interrelated with each other because both aim to maximize productivity by eliminating wastes and wasteful practices.

"5 Pillars of the Visual Workplace" also offers a number of significant and related case studies that include 5S training materials and graphic demonstrations and illustrations.

"New Manufacturing Challenge"

This book details and outlines the competitive techniques and strategies successfully implemented and adopted by successful and giant global companies in the past two decades.

Authored by another Japanese researcher, Kiyoshi Suzaki, "New Manufacturing Challenge" focuses on manufacturing firms and provides recommendations on how these companies can boost production efficiency.

"New Manufacturing Challenge" is very much recommended specifically for manufacturing and production specialists.

"Just Another Car Factory?"

The book is written by Christopher Huxley, James Rinehart and David Robertson.

"Just Another Car Factory?" demonstrates the effective implementation and use of lean manufacturing techniques by taking the example of the CAMI Automotive.

CAMI Automotive is a joint car making business of US-based General Motors and Japan's Suzuki. It is understood that CAMI Automotive has developed and adopted one of the most effective lean production facilities.

By taking a closer look and conducting a case study of the company, the authors have successfully come up with a book that touches mainly on lean manufacturing, including the aspects of sociology, labor, human resources management and industrial relations.

"Lean Manufacturing Implementation"

"Lean Manufacturing Implementation" is a sequential and step-by-step informative reading about implementation of lean manufacturing techniques in businesses.

The lean manufacturing book is authored by Dennis Hobbs and co-published by CPIM and APICS. "Lean Manufacturing Implementation" was published in October 2003.

The book enumerates comprehensible and understandable transformation of manufacturing businesses into productive ones using lean manufacturing techniques.

"Lean Manufacturing Implementation" is written in a manner that readers will surely easily understand the techniques and description due to the simple words, vocabularies and sentence structures used by the author.

"Lean Manufacturing Implementation" also tackles common problems and concerns arising from the implementation of lean manufacturing techniques as well as effective and recommended solutions to address these lean manufacturing issues.

"What is Lean Six Sigma"

"What is Lean Six Sigma" is written by Bill Kastle, David T Rowlands and Michael George.

This lean manufacturing book focuses on the integration of the Lean Six Sigma, which practically and effectively combines the principles of improving work (through the use of the paradigm of the so-called workplace Six Sigma) and faster work (through using and implementing key lean manufacturing principles).

"What is Lean Six Sigma" will surely be an easy reading, but informative, because the authors employed the plain-English style of book writing.

Lean Manufacturing Consultants

The world of manufacturing has always been driven to be effective and efficient at the same time, this is where the lean manufacturing consultant comes in.

This type of consultant is very proficient in using various techniques and tools that can really and most often and not significantly improve the manufacturing business.

Every business wants to be streamlined. Applying lean principles will depends on the lean manufacturing consultant. There are other factors to consider. If the company is already applying different lean principles, it might want to implement another lean tool aside from the ones that they already are using. If the business has not made use of a lean manufacturing consultant, they will have to start from the basics and move on from there.

Lean manufacturing consultants having a new company to which they will be applying the lean principles for the first time have to get the changes right the first time. These changes start from the base of the business, and not getting it right can have serious consequences.

What do lean manufacturing consultants really do? Why is their job so important in the manufacturing business? Lean manufacturing consultants first look at your current business process. Through analysis of your business processes, they can determine which changes to make and thus improve your business even more like for time to manufacture the product, to it's delivery and of course profit.

To focus on how the lean manufacturing consultant will improve your business, we will give a breakdown of what he does. First we have to know what is a process. A process is doing an action or a series of actions and getting a reaction.

For example the process of preparing cup noodles. You have to open up the cup noodles, then put hot water up to a certain point, Cover the cup noodle and wait for 3 minutes. This is in itself a process. To sum it up, everything we do everyday is a process.

Lean Manufacturing Principles Made Easy

A lean manufacturing consultant for a company has to first select a process. He has to then document on how this process is done. To be able to do this he has to sit down and talk it over with the people that are involved in this task and list every detail that they tell him. A good thing to do here is to make use of a flowchart to show the steps that the process makes.

After documenting the work process, the lean manufacturing consultant has to analyze it. You have to time how long each process takes to finish. Then pinpoint the important and not so important steps, if the step repeats or does not repeat itself. You will then have an idea of how long and where to improve on the current business process.

The lean manufacturing consultant's next task is to implement the necessary changes to improve the business process. Talking to the management here is very important since you need their support in having your new business process put into action.

Not having the support of the management will have made your work a waste. What's more, the company will not have improved on that area or process which you have analyzed.

The lean manufacturing consultant also has to scrutinize the important steps that have been identified before to see if there is anyway in improving them or if they have become not important and can be done without.

This process is repeated over and over again until the lean manufacturing consultant has gone through all the processes of the business. After making use of the expertise of a lean manufacturing consultant, I'm sure that your business will have aside from better profit, less waste, more productivity, a better management employee relationship, better benefits, and of course a streamlined efficient business for the owner. All this courtesy of the lean manufacturing consultant.

Hiring the right lean manufacturing consultant can also spell the difference of a successful lean management implementation and the death of an organization. A lean manufacturing consultant must be very knowledgeable and has the experience to handle the different processes of different types of organization.

The lean manufacturing consultant must be able to predict trends and yet establish a standardization process within the company to make sure that there is no wasted resource. This is why a lean manufacturing consultant is highly prized by any organization.

Implementing The Lean Manufacturing Strategy

Before we discuss how to implement the much discussed corporate planning strategy known as lean manufacturing, let us first define what it is.

Lean manufacturing is a combination of approaches that, when put together, aims to eliminate the all the common practices that are seen as wholly unnecessary and time-consuming. Such are called wastes, like overproduction, long waiting times, transportation and constant motion, which not only eat up precious time but are also a drag on resources, energy and expenses.

Simply put, implementing lean manufacturing has the reduction of costs in mind. And this is done, ironically, by first making sacrifices on the strategies that have been in effect in many companies for decades now.

Sound like a dangerous plan? Some companies believe it is, but when you really look at its long term benefits, you will find that implementing lean manufacturing will bring greater value to your company than the processes that have already been ingrained. After all, change is often for the better. You just have to open your eyes and welcome it.

Implementing the lean manufacturing program is best for companies that have output and production as their primary source of revenue. Such companies place a prime on maximizing all their human and tool resources in order to achieve their target output levels without having to spend too much.

This is where the principles of lean manufacturing are most helpful.

Prevailing economic conditions often leave companies scampering for clients. Growing competition are forcing producers to lower their charges just to be able to get ahead, that's why such firms are looking for novel ways to lower their production costs and increase turnaround times. When firms need to boost efficiencies and generate revenue, lean manufacturing is often what is implemented.

Lean Manufacturing Principles Made Easy

Implementing lean manufacturing techniques has been found effective in the survival and success of a company or an organization. This is because of the 'elimination of seven wastes' philosophy this program espouses.

For a shorter version, what lean manufacturing aims to teach is the on time, at the right time and at the right quantity approach to production. For instance, producing too much that what is needed is often detrimental to a company. Sure, it shows that targets have not only been achieved, but grossly surpassed. But this does not always entail success.

Implementing lean manufacturing systems means that there should no waste. That is, no unnecessary stockpiles that could just sit at warehouses and left to rot. If you produce more than intended, this is what will likely happen to your inventory.

You'll take up warehouse space and see the products get worn by time. If you're lucky, you'll be able to dispose of the excesses, but they won't likely be sold at their original price because, well, they'll be considered old stocks or overruns.

Before you plan to implement lean manufacturing strategies, it's best to be prepared. Critics are not kidding when they say that lean manufacturing is somewhat tricky, because the preliminary preparations can, indeed, deter you from pushing through.

However, consider the long term gains you will obtain from this system. If you list pros and cons, you will find that the benefits will significantly outweigh the tedious preparations and planning by a long shot. Once you've laid down what needs to be changed and what needs to be eliminated, implementing should be a piece of cake.

Good luck!

Lean Manufacturing Printing Industry

The printing industry, just like all other global industries, is also affected by the crunches and economic hardships affecting global corporate firms nowadays.

The printing industry is mostly affected now by the rising popularity of the internet. The broadcast industry, for the past few decades have dominated the whole media universe.

That is why when revenues of broadcast companies started falling in the past couple of years, people and companies around the world were taken in awe and disbelief.

Why? because the present people, probably including you, have grown up sitting in front of the television. People in these times have grown and become TV addicts.

For decades, TV has dominated and taken most of the advertising revenues. The radio industry has taken the second pie of the chart and the printing industry the least market and advertising share.

Hard times for the printing industry:

Obviously, the printing industry is the hardest hit by the emergence of the internet. The least ad revenue share once enjoyed by the printing industry is now made even smaller.

All the companies around the world are living out the hardest of all times today. The printing industry is sure the hardest hit by the popularity of the online media.

Revenues and profits of printing industry firms are significantly falling and declining. That is why every month, you probably are hearing or reading news about job cuts, mergers and acquisitions, bankruptcy and selling off of many companies that belong to the printing industry.

It is basically the hardest time for the printing industry. It is most of all made worse by the current economic events and problems that are not unique to the printing industry.

Lean Manufacturing:

Companies from around the world, from all industries, are now adopting the techniques and principles of lean manufacturing.

Lean manufacturing refers to the set of strategies and techniques implemented in the work place that aim to reduce, significantly cut down, operating costs and expenses of companies.

There are seven identified wastes that lean manufacturing intends to eliminate in the work place. These seven are identified as: over processing, over production, motion, transportation, waiting, inventory and scrap and defects.

Each waste contributes to the losses the companies incur with much quantity. Quality of outputs of companies are also lessened and sacrificed. What is worse is that competitiveness is much affected also. Indeed, the prevailing time is characterized by the cliché "survival of the fittest."

Lean Manufacturing and the print industry

Lean manufacturing may be the last hope for the printing industry. Because of the promises, the forecast and expected savings companies can reap from implementing lean manufacturing principles: the printing industry is believed to be the most and primarily boosted and lifted up by the lean manufacturing approaches.

The printing industry has somehow turned into a damsel in distress. With the lean manufacturing, figuratively, its knight in shining armor.

The manufacturing industry is benefiting from the gains and advantages of the adoption of lean manufacturing techniques. The printing industry, obviously, will also have the same gains some experts believe there will be much more.

It is about time printing industries now implement lean manufacturing techniques on it's own. For sure, lean manufacturing adoption will not make the printing industry outpace or displace the online industry. But one thing is for sure.

Lean manufacturing will surely help print industry players last and out live its destiny. It is said that printing industry is not meant to last longer. It can be true because the time and technologies have evolved along with people's preferences and interests.

The printing industry surely needs its redemption factor. This is the opportunity it has been waiting all along. The opportunity to generate savings reduces operational costs and improve efficiency and competitiveness, all rolled into one single package. Lean manufacturing is the best means to lift up the printing industry.

Lean Manufacturing Six Sigma

Both lean manufacturing and six sigma are management philosophies or tools that help a company eliminate wastefulness in manufacturing and other types of industry.

Because the times are changing, processes advancing and needs intensifying, more and more companies face challenges as regards their efficiency and profitability. And both lean manufacturing and six sigma introduce solutions to these dilemmas, without putting much strain on a firm's energy and resources.

Lean manufacturing

Lean manufacturing has been proven to significantly aid in the streamlining of operations and reduction of waste. It welcomes the concept of continuously raising the value added to a certain business activity or method via the reduction of the so-called seven wastes: namely, transportation, motion, overproduction, inventory, over processing, scrap and defects and waiting time.

What lean manufacturing does is provide implementing firms with adequate tools to make it in the increasingly competitive global market, which is everyday faster turnaround times, higher quality and lower prices.

Here are some advantages of lean manufacturing:

- lean manufacturing strengthens production processes
- lean manufacuring significantly lower the chain of wasteful activities and resources
- lean manufacturing increases flexibility by improving layouts
- lean manufacturing reduces floor space needs and inventory dramatically, and
- lean manufacturing introduces and implements more appropriate and up-to-date delivery systems

Six Sigma

The six sigma management philosophy, like lean manufacturing, is also tailored to reduce waste, but it is more focused on eliminating waste linked with production method or equipment defects.

The tools under six sigma are used by firms to further improve and develop a company's products and systems, via the consolidation of engineering, business and statistical data. As with lean manufacturing, six sigma can also be applied to any form of corporation or organization, whether engaged in the services, marketing, design, sales or production industries.

Some advantages delivered by the six sigma management tool:

- six sigma improves and boost a firm's systems and products
- six sigma reduces the chain of wastes
- six sigma lessens costs by around 50% via self-financed methods
- six sigma easily adapts to changer customer tastes
- six sigma drives growth using the internal resources available to it

What both philosophies do is help firms dramatically increase their productivity by around 75% to 125% because they ensure that no time, energy or resource is wasted in any of the processing levels. To put it in simple terms, both lean manufacturing and six sigma are bent on nipping problems at the bud, or, even nipping problems before they occur.

A vigilant approach to business is what companies need nowadays to be able to cope with the fast changing times. Sure, while some systems have worked for us for decades now, it wouldn't hurt to try something that is relatively new and proven to be so much better at delivering positive results.

The Benefits Of A Lean Manufacturing System

A lean manufacturing system is a system and philosophy that was first developed by Toyota for its production system. Lots of manufacturing business has adopted this system for them to enjoy the benefits that it has to offer.

The name "lean manufacturing system" is a generic term that refers to the principles and theories to rid your business of waste. Waste in a lean manufacturing system is referred to processes that do not add to the value for money for the customer that buys from you.

The lean manufacturing system principles are:

1. Value - Customer's willingness to pay for your product.

2. Value Stream – Add-ons to a product or process.

3. Flow - The movement of your product being biased to single piece flow or work cells rather than production lines.

4. Pull - Having the right amount of materials to manufacture the product at the same time having a small or no inventory.

5. Continuous Improvement - Getting rid of waste on a constant basis.

For example, if you order a computer over the Internet it may take a week for your computer to be delivered to you. It will only take a few hours for the technician to assemble and have your computer ready for use.

The reason why it may take a week is because of the different shipping practices used by the company. It may also be bottlenecks within their current manufacturing system like having the company wait for the required materials to arrive that make you wait those extra days.

Lean Manufacturing Principles Made Easy

Having a lean manufacturing system for your business and the application of its various principles can make your order for a new computer shorter. Instead of waiting for a week for your computer to be delivered to you, it may just take 24 to 48 hours. The lean manufacturing system is designed to give the customer value for money at the lowest price at the least given time.

Another good example of a lean manufacturing system is the eyeglasses in an hour. Usually it would take at least 24 hours for glasses to be made and delivered to the customer, maybe even longer. A lot of lean principles have been applied to this lean manufacturing system. Now you see a lot of eyeglasses in an hour stores from malls to stores near your street.

Judging from the examples above you may think that the quickness in delivery is the only benefit that a lean manufacturing system can give a business. Actually this is just one in the many benefits that having a lean manufacturing system can offer. A lean manufacturing system also gets rid of waste while maintaining low cost and at the same time satisfying customer needs.

Getting rid of waste and all the useless processes is so crucial to the lean manufacturing system that it even has it's own term "muda." "Muda" in lean manufacturing system is also a Japanese word for waste.

There are seven types of considered waste in the lean manufacturing system:

1. Over Production - Producing a product that is made faster than is sold is wasteful.

2. Inventory - A product that has to be stored is wasteful because it ties up money as inventory.

3. Conveyance - Moving a part unnecessarily during production is wasteful. Can also damage the part.

4. Correction - Having to inspect, correct your products because of production errors is a huge waste of time and money. This can be overcome with error proofing. This means that the product can be made through that way only.

5. Motion - Awkward movements of the operator can put different aches on different parts of their body. Making this area better will reduce injury and workman injury claims.

6. Processing - Customer requirements that are not clear to the manufacturer cause the manufacturer to produce different add-ons that is wasteful since it will increase the cost of the product.

7. Waiting - The operator doing nothing is a waste. It's ok that the machine waits for the operator not the other way around.

Eliminating waste through lean manufacturing system streamlines your company thus by getting more done with less equipment, capital, space, effort, labor, inventory and time.

Having a lean manufacturing system established in a company's organization could do wonders. This is because while saving time, money and precious resource, the company's production system is improved and becomes more efficient. Other companies admire this attribute that to have a lean manufacturing system can only mean a good management.

Move Ahead The Corporate Ladder With Lean Manufacturing Training

In a business setting that operates under lean manufacturing principles, it is important that the staff and employees of the company must have lean manufacturing training. Lean manufacturing is a management principle that almost every business wants to emulate. Lean manufacturing is all about reducing waste to make the business more effective and efficient.

Lean manufacturing training begins with the classroom setting with managers, consultant, implementers and employees are gathered to learn the concepts, formulate programs and create worthwhile solutions to the company's inefficiencies. The lean manufacturing training consultants may ask the staff to divide into teams.

Forming teams within the corporate system is very important in lean manufacturing training. Lean manufacturing philosophy depends on the correlation of the units is a large organization and the cause and effect of each person in the unit. When lean manufacturing training begins, the value of having team pride is expressed.

Teams undergoing lean manufacturing training cover a lot of areas from statistical Process Control, Team Building, Job Skills and Root Cause Analysis. Often during their training, many are shy and are reserved with their ideas. They lack the confidence in their work and don't really feel a part of something greater.

When they finish with their lean manufacturing training, all their inhibitions are set aside. Their lean manufacturing training makes them more competent in their jobs as a team and individuals. Giving these people a vision or attainable goal helps give them pride in them and their work.

During the lean manufacturing training, destructive and emotional conflict during work is turned into constructive brainstorming and problem solving. The lean manufacturing training sharpens the managers' decision-making abilities through case studies. Employees and managers see eye to eye on internal issues and their lean manufacturing training encourages them to think outside the box as a whole team when problems arise.

One of the major benefits of undergoing lean manufacturing training is the satisfaction of getting the job done. It gives pride to the team who solves it and helps make the company more efficient. By involving the entry-level staff to the managers in attaining realistic goals set within a timeframe, they are encouraged to give their best.

Another benefit is that the company stands to gain more from the lean manufacturing training. With the company's production processes becoming efficient without sacrificing the quality and quantity of the goods and services, more profits are expected to come in.

The lean manufacturing training also teaches the managers how to spot wastes within the system. Since zero waste is the a must in the implementation of lean manufacturing, learning to identify what works and what doesn't in a department is a valuable trait for anyone wishing to climb the corporate ladder.

It's all about being smart and effective as an individual. Eventually, the door of opportunity will open once you've taken the lean manufacturing training to heart.

Lean manufacturing training for the different groups in a company

There are six groups that may be involved in the implementation of the lean manufacturing philosophy in a company. Because of the different level in the role of each group, lean manufacturing training for each of them also differs.

1. Executive Management – this group is responsible for establishing the culture of zero waste in all the departments. They are the ones everyone expects to set the bar for exemplary lean manufacturing training. Because of this, their training covers a lot of the philosophy of lean manufacturing and how to integrate its principles in the company's way of business.

2. Lean masters – this is a selected group of highly qualified company experts on lean management that are trained to become leaders in advancing the lean management plans. They are usually selected within the company and their lean manufacturing training is all about getting results.

3. **Middle Management** – this group is tasked with the responsibility of identifying opportunities within the company. They also must be able to prioritize which projects need more attention and how to achieve the results expected from the projects. Their lean manufacturing training is more focused on the production process of the company.

4. **Lean Implementation Teams** – this group is directly responsible for implementing the lean manufacturing tools throughout the organization. Their lean manufacturing training is requires them to have a good understanding of the lean tools to fulfill their directives.

5. **Office Support** – this group only undergoes lean manufacturing training when their actions can directly help in the success of the lean project. Often, they do not have to take the lean manufacturing training.

With lean manufacturing training, everyone in the company can become a valuable resource. And by helping create a leaner more efficient workplace, the company can be expected to last for a very long time, which means more jobs and opportunities for promotion to its employees.

The Philosophy Of Lean Manufacturing

In the field of management, there are various approaches that principally aim to accelerate and boost corporate firms' revenues and operational efficiencies.

Progressive companies from around the world have been coming up every now and then different strategies for corporate improvement. Some of these schemes have been so effective that other firms have recognized and even adopted them.

One of these efficiency-focused philosophies is what is termed 'lean manufacturing.'

What is lean manufacturing?

Lean manufacturing is a holistic and strategic approach that aims to enable businesses and companies to improve and boost competitiveness and profitability.

Lean manufacturing aims to introduce and set in desired improvements through identifying, and gradually, eliminating wasteful or unproductive behavior and practices among employees and management.

The scheme called lean manufacturing is a program or methodology that could prove to be fitting and appropriate for all types of businesses or organizations. Lean manufacturing would be effective whether adopted by companies in the manufacturing, service, trading or other sectors.

Lean manufacturing is focused at helping companies get the right things, to the right and appropriate places, at the perfect or right time and in the right amount or quantity while at the same time, reducing waste and promoting productivity and flexibility among workers.

Lean manufacturing and wastes

It does not take a successful manager to assert that businesses and companies carry unnecessary and unlikely burden of wastes.

Lean Manufacturing Principles Made Easy

Lean manufacturing as a philosophy focuses on reducing the seven wastes commonly identified among global firms. Lean manufacturing attempts to help companies eliminate these unnecessary wastes to improve output quality, to maximize production and the time needed for it and mostly, to significantly save on costs.

The seven wastes lean manufacturing aims to slash and eliminate in the workplace are the following:

1. Over production
2. Over processing
3. Transportation
4. Motion
5. Inventory
6. Waiting
7. Scrap and defects

Over production, over processing and inventory

While some companies view over production in the positive way, most, especially those in the service and manufacturing sectors, take it as a manufacturing liability.

Over production will create a piling of inventory that would eventually create a problem in distribution because most warehouses have capacity limits.

What is worse is that over production and piling of inventories are the usual causes of price drops, which are deemed bad for the business by most firms.

The fundamental law of supply and demand will attest that if supplies are exceeding or too much, the demand tries to settle down or decline. Demands going down will mean prices rolling back or dropping as well.

Over processing is unnecessary because it takes so much productive time from employees and managers. There are many disadvantage of over processing and most of them seem pretty obvious to you. Over processing makes costs blow up.

Transportation, motion and waiting

Because time is an important element of productivity, lean manufacturing values it the most. Thus, lean manufacturing philosophy aims to boost efficiency.

Transportation is an essential element of manufacturing because through it commodities and merchandise are distributed to retailers, down to the consumers.

However, lean manufacturing mandates firms to maximize the use of transportation especially nowadays when oil prices are soaring.

Because energy prices are rising, and energy is what makes companies rolling, motion should be controlled. Lean manufacturing will have companies slash procrastination and unproductive hours among employees so as to increase and meet sufficient production targets.

If motion is made efficient, then waiting could be reduced if not eliminated. In lean manufacturing, waiting makes idle of people and it kills time that should have been used instead in productive measures and activities.

Scrap and defects

Lean manufacturing have it that if employees are efficient and if they are motivated, the quality of production would be greatly boosted. That means, the company will not have to spend costs on wages, energies and other capital just to produce defective items that would eventually rejected upon distribution.

While scraps and defects in production items are inevitable, companies adhering to lean manufacturing could always do something about it. Basic management principles have it that motivation is the most effective incentive to get workers doing the right and proper procedures in the work place.

All the seven wastes that are combated by lean manufacturing strategies are somehow interconnected with each other that eliminating one could lead to the elimination of the others.

What Is Lean Manufacturing?

Today, in a highly consumerist society where people strive to acquire more possessions, it is ironic that in manufacturing consumer products, lean is in.

The concept of zero-waste does not only circulate among ecological zones, it seems. Lean manufacturing is a new buzzword in the industrial world which is rapidly gaining ubiquitous following. Lean manufacturing is a systematic approach to eliminate waste in the production process with the end goal of satisfying customers.

Waste is anything that a consumer refuses to pay for. The types of wastes in a manufacturing system include the following:

(a) overproduction or producing more, earlier or faster than required
(b) waiting for machines to process
(c) inventory or work in process because of large lot production or processes with long cycle time
(d) unnecessary processing
(e) transportation which hardly adds values to products
(f) excessive motion of workers, machines and transport due to inappropriate location of tools and parts
(g) making defective products and
(h) underutilizing people.

The focus of lean manufacturing is to minimize the consumption of resources that adds no value to a product. As such, it is a process-focused production system which minimizes costs, maximizes customer options and ensures high quality and fast delivery of products and services.

The concept of lean manufacturing originated in Japan where, after WWII, it was necessary for manufacturers to develop a new, low cost manufacturing process.

Lean Manufacturing Principles Made Easy

Unlike their western counterparts, Japanese manufacturers needed to rebuild after the war and faced declining human, material and financial resources. The first leaders to create lean manufacturing systems were Eiji Toyoda, Taiichi Ohno and Shingeo Shingo of Toyota Motor Company.

In the 1990's, the concept of lean manufacturing was popularized in the U.S. by a study conducted by the Massachusetts Institute of Technology on the movement of mass production toward the more streamlined Japanese production style as described in the book entitled The Machine That Changed the World (Womack, Jones & Ross).

This depicted essential elements which are used in lean manufacturing systems. The term lean was adopted because these methods used less human effort, capital investment, production space, materials and time in all operation stages.

All U.S. manufacturing businesses eventually applied lean manufacturing because of competition among U.S. and Japanese automakers over the last two decades.

Lean manufacturing systems recognize the fact that the value of a product is defined solely by the customer. Customers' needs must be met at a specific time and price. The nitty-gritty of product operations is of no importance to customers.

This realization forces companies to comprehensively analyze business processes.

To apply lean manufacturing is to understand basic activities required to produce a particular product and to optimize the entire process from the point of view of the customer. This is important as it helps identify activities that clearly add value, those have no value-added and cannot be avoided and those that have no value-added and can be scrapped altogether.

Transition to a lean manufacturing system does not happen overnight. Lean manufacturing requires every level of organization to have a complete understanding of its basic principles and execution processes. Widespread orientations must be set to prepare and motivate people and to make them understand the need to switch to lean manufacturing.

After that, a mentality for continuous improvement is necessary to reach company goals. This means that the company aims for incremental improvement of products, and processes over time.

For this, employee involvement and an atmosphere of experimentation are essential. Decision-making and system development must be delegated. Willingness to take risks must be encouraged.

Improvements must be measured according to results vis-à-vis macro level targets not on number of activities undertaken. Because of the complicated nature of lean manufacturing systems, there is a need to execute pilot projects before spreading the culture across the organization.

The number of manufacturers attempting to become lean is increasing fast. Companies that have fully implemented lean manufacturing systems are rare. Although perfection is impossible, it is a goal that lean manufacturers strive for because it helps them be more vigilant of wasteful practices.

The Lean Manufacturing Process

Lean manufacuring process is a general term for a wide variety of manufacturing methodologies that are bent on maximizing the value and minimizing the waste in a manufacturing process.

The lean manufacturing process had its origin from the Toyota Production System in Japan. Most of the pharses and terms used in the lean manufacturing process such as kanban, kaizen and andon are Japanese terms that became standards in teh lean manufacturing process.

The Focus Of Lean Manufacturing

Basically, lean manufacturing is focused on value. What is value?

Value is defined in the lean manufacturing process as something that the customer is willing to pay for. Aside from this, all aspects of the manufacturing process is now deemed a waste.

So all processes that is included in the lean manufacturing process is focused on gaining value and reducing waste. The lean manufacturing process is seen as a tool that focuses all the resources and energies to the features with value and less on the features with no value.

Lean Manufacturing Process Is Customer Centric

Lean manufacturing process is customer centric. The term value that is defined in the lean manufacturing process is based on the definition of value from a customer's point of view.

Companies who have identified their customers and how they define the term value will focus all their resources on that particular value.

So basically, companies who observe lean manufacturing processes are manufacturing based on customer needs.

Through the use of lean manufacturing process, companies hopes to satisfy their customers and gain more revenue.

Lean Manufacturing Process Eliminates Waste

The lean manufacturing process eliminates waste. Waste is defined in the lean manufacturing process as anything that the customer is not willing to pay for.

So companies hoped for eliminating waste by conserving the process in manufacturing. Companies focuses on correcting the levels of quality and features of the manufacturing process. The companies hopes to make the manufacturing process "leaner" by eliminating unnecessary processes or loops.

In a lean manufacturing process, an inventory that is depleted is simply replenished, when a customer demands, the company delivers the product, all processes are monitored and checked.

Upon monitoring, the company will be able to have standard targets and will have an idea whenever the manufacturing process has reached its qouta or is higher or below what is expectant of it.

These figures will also tell the company of any loopholes that it needs to correct. By correcting these loopholes and avoiding any unnecessary items in the process, the process will be faster and more effective.

Basically, the equation for the actual cost of a product has changed since the advent of the lean manufacturing process. Previously, the equation is price of the product is equal to the cost of manufacturing and the expectant profit.

After implementing the lean manufacturing process, the equation is still the same but was seen in a different view. The profit is now equal to the sales price of the product minus the cost of manufacturing.

Lean Manufacturing Process Is Continuous Improvement

The lean manufacturing process also commits to the continuous improvement of the manufacturing line. Doing so will eliminate whatever process that can be eliminated as time passes by. Old processes will always be replaced by newer and better ones.

The lean manufacturing process is always open for changes and adjustments. As time passes by, more and more automation of processes will make the manufacturing process shorter and more robust.

Lean Manufacturing Process Is Effective

All in all, the objective of the lean manufacturing process is to satisfy the customers, increase the morale of the employees, and increase the gain of the shareholders.

The lean manufacturing process satisfies the customers because it provide their needs and deliver them on time. The lean manufacturing process satisfies the employees of the companies because it eliminates unnecessary and tiring process along the manufacturing line. Also, more and more automation of the processes will surely eliminate any human error along the process.

The lean manufacturing process satisfies the shareholders because it hopes to implement continuous improvements along the manufacturing line. The manufacturing process will be more effective and the company will have more revenue gain from this. More and more products will be able to be manufactured and yet the quality of the product is not tainted.

Learning The Basics Of Lean Manufacturing And Processing

Lean manufacturing and processing has been an important strategy and basic technique in helping companies improve their profitability and competitiveness.

The fundamental function of lean manufacturing and processing is to reduce wastes and unnecessary work practices and behaviors among workers of a particular manufacturing company.

Because the times have really gone hard, demanding and intense due to political and turbulent concerns affecting all nations, firms are currently facing challenges to be able to keep their profitability and efficiency.

In principle, there are seven identified 'forms of waste' within the work environment and systems that lean manufacturing and processing principally aims to alleviate, if not totally eliminate. These are over production, over processing, transportation, motion, inventory, waiting and scrap and defects.

Lean manufacturing and processing principles not only reduce operational costs but also aims to boost, restore and drastically improve the competitiveness of a troubled or struggling, even already good-performing, company.

That is basically why learning about lean manufacturing and processing has somehow become imperative for major and global companies.

The era of complete globalization is at hand. That contributes more pressure for companies to start acting right away to be able to survive the rough and hard operational and company challenges ahead.

Lean manufacturing and processing

Lean manufacturing and processing surely gets companies moving along and enjoying huge benefits of really reducing operational costs. If savings are generated, the saved amounts can be used for further capital requirements and investments that could further help companies expand and grow organically.

Lean manufacturing and processing, however, is not very easy to implement and adopt. The companies involved should really and religiously pay particular attention to details to be able to ensure the success of the efforts.

The number of companies adopting lean manufacturing and processing principles is surely and is apparently on the rise, no doubt about that.

But the thing is, firms adopting lean manufacturing and processing techniques are most of the time, not achieving target and aimed results because they are not doing the strategies and techniques properly.

Insufficient and ineffective implementation of lean manufacturing and processing principles and techniques will surely make the companies' efforts and capital infusion for the initiative futile and wasted.

It should be noted, also, that lean manufacturing and processing principles would not stand on its own. Companies adopting and embracing them should also strive harder to attain their goals.

Learn about lean manufacturing and processing

Experts advise companies to really get involved in and further learn more about lean manufacturing and processing. It is a logical and surely beneficial effort because lean manufacturing and processing can surely help companies get on with the current challenges and concerns affecting all firms around the world.

There are many ways on how companies can get to learn more about lean manufacturing and processing principles and techniques.

For one, they can hire lean manufacturing and processing experts and professionals who are credible and knowledgeable on the subject and who can really help the companies attain and maximize the benefits of such strategies.

However, hiring lean manufacturing and processing professionals will entail additional costs and investments from companies. They should not really mind it, because the benefits from lean manufacturing and processing implementation will surely offset the little and minimal costs of learning it.

Another thing, companies can designate key personnel to specifically and intently learn lean manufacturing and processing principles and techniques.

It is a common practice by companies around the world currently. The arrangement sees the key personnel attends seminars and get books to really know or learn the lean manufacturing and processing principles.

After that, the designated and assigned personnel will relay the message and everything he learned to the whole staff. It is up to him whether he will make the learning process for his officemates fast-paced or low-paced.

What is important is that the skills and knowledge are distributed and communicated to the entire organization. That way, lean manufacturing and processing principles are really and seriously imbibed by all personnel, to make the strategies work overall for the company.

Lean manufacturing and processing should be learned by all companies because the benefits it assures them, is nothing compared to the costs of absorbing them, which are not really that significant.

Wise, isn't it?

When Is A Change In Management Required In Lean Manufacturing?

The Wikipedia Website defines lean manufacturing as a management issue or philosophy that focuses on the elimination, if not reduction, of the seven wastes.

The so-called seven wastes are identified by labor experts as the factors, both huge and little, that effect or influence the profitability of the given company.

You know that companies spend most of their capital on investments, equipment and work force. The investments are expected to generate revenues, which in turn decide on whether the company will keep afloat.

The seven wastes that companies find as burdens to their production and existence are defeats, motion, inventory, over processing, transportation, waiting time and over production.

The seven wastes

As mentioned, the seven wastes are the usual factors that are blamed for the losses and demise of modern-day companies. The seven wastes, as you might have noticed, are somehow directly linked to the companies' working culture and environment.

Over production make up for filing of inventories, which is not necessary and negatively related to production because as supplies increase, prices do fall or decrease, as stated in the law of supply and demand.

Over processing and slow motion result in longer wasting time, which makes companies unproductive. Motion of personnel is disturbed and made slower when there lots of equipments not used in the workplace that obviously make free movement hard.

You know that when people can move freely, they can get to do more activities and accomplish more tasks.

Defects and scraps in outputs can be prevented along with all the wastes. The seven wastes also involve and cover behavioral patterns of employees, which can negatively affect the overall being of the company.

Lean manufacturing advantages

There are numerous advantages and benefits enumerated from the implementation of lean manufacturing principles.

For one, savings are consequently generated, and revenues and incomes are rapidly and effectively improved. Savings will mean a lot to a company because capital is so hard to raise nowadays and operation factors and inputs are becoming more and more expensive.

Competition nowadays has also gone so intense that all companies, whether from different industries or not, are practically up against each others' sleeves. Competitiveness is another aspect of the companies that lean manufacturing aims to cover.

To help cope up with the intense rivalry and competition among companies, lean manufacturing aims to boost production and quality credibility. These two factors are very essential when it comes to improving sales through active and good relations with customers and consumers.

The management and lean manufacturing

So one important question involving the adoption of lean manufacturing techniques is, " when is management revamped or changed resulting from the implementation of lean manufacturing techniques?

The answer to the question can somehow get hard and complex. To seek answers for the above mentioned interrogative statement would also be equally complicated and will require too thorough probing and searching.

Lean manufacturing principally aims to rationalize and streamline operations of companies. Experts argue that the process does not necessarily require a change in management.

But it can be noted that the distinct features of almost all companies under lean manufacturing initiatives are the change and revamp in management. The subject is the main cause of stress nowadays among executives and directors.

It can be safe and logical to assert, however, that because lean manufacturing entails the elimination of wasteful practices and behaviors in the workplace that some executives are axed. It can be ironic that several board seats and top posts are onlygreat wastes of capital and compensation packages.

Lean manufacturing advisor recommend a change in management to most effectively make the adoption of lean manufacturing principles really work.

The Five Principles Of Lean Manufacturing

All companies seek ways to improve their businesses. One of the most common goals of trumping the competition is cutting expenses, which can be best achieved through lean manufacturing strategies.

But before anything, let us first define what lean manufacturing is. Lean manufacturing is a management concept that supports the 'no waste' policy. These 'wastes' refer to the seven most common reasons for underproductivity and delay identified by companies all over the world.

They are inventory, over production, waiting time, transportation, processing, scrap and defects and motion. According to studies, most firms waste between 70% and 90% of the resources available to them. These happen when there are huge stockpiles of overruns, or when it takes ten activity levels to achieve something that can be done equally as good as when completed in three steps. The list can go on, but you get the picture.

The tricky part about implementing lean manufacturing principles is that most of the wastes identified are invisible, making their reduction and eventual eradication challenging. But with careful planning, lean manufacturing should be a walk in the park for your company

There are five core disciplines in lean manufacturing. Not all firms require their implementation, but at least one of which is necessary for the betterment, or 'leaning', of an organization.

1) team development
2) cellular manufacturing
3) six sigma and total quality management
4) rapid setup
5) pull scheduling

To complement the above, the following five lean manufacturing principles are what serve as guidelines for firms that want to maximize value out of their organization.

Out With Waste

Lean manufacturing principles focus on eliminating waste from the company. This means taking out unnecessary departments or redundant positions, or eradicating processes that just cause delay.

If it means terminating jobs, then do so. Lean manufacturing espouses that all resources, land, persons and capital, are used in the best and most efficient way they can be used.

Do It Right The First Time

Trial and error methods are simply a waste of resources and time. If enough effort is placed in carefully planning a certain manufacturing process, then there wouldn't be the need to start all over again, or settle with mediocre situations.

Always Seek The Best

Every company should always reach for the highest value that can be achieved. All the effort will be futile and major waste if this isn't done so.

Be Flexible

Lean manufacturing principles do not support stiff and linear thinking. If something needs to be improved and changed along the way, then do so at once, instead of contending with the original plan that has been eventually found to be resource and time-wasteful along the way.

Don't Push, Pull

Consumers should be given the freedom to decide what they want. As a manufacturer, you should impose trends or products to your clients. Rather, you should always be on the lookout for what will make your consumers happy.

Of course, adopting lean manufacturing principles does not always mean that your company is saved. It still takes careful planning, method-mapping and a lot of discipline to succeed. If your company is not wary of the consequences of strategies that are haphazardly implemented, then these lean manufacturing principles will be in vain -- and total waste.

This Product Is Brought To You By

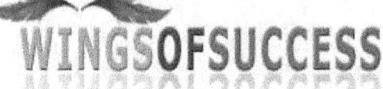

www.ingramcontent.com/pod-product-compliance
Lightning Source LLC
LaVergne TN
LVHW020430080526
838202LV00055B/5105